TWO BLACK BUFFALO

First edition
published in 2009 by

WOODFIELD PUBLISHING LTD
Bognor Regis ~ West Sussex ~ England ~ PO21 5EL
www.woodfieldpublishing.co.uk

© Imre Istvan Koller, 2009

The right of Imre Istvan Koller
to be identified as Author of this work
has been asserted in accordance with
the Copyright, Designs and Patents Act 1988

ISBN 1-84683-089-3

Two Black Buffalo

The true story of a young Hungarian boy who survived against all odds

IMRE ISTVAN KOLLER

Woodfield

Woodfield Publishing Ltd

Woodfield House ~ Babsham Lane ~ Bognor Regis ~ West Sussex ~ PO21 5EL
telephone 01243 821234 ~ **e-mail** enquiries@woodfieldpublishing.co.uk

Interesting and informative books on a variety of subjects

For full details of all our published titles, visit our website at
www.woodfieldpublishing.com

This book is dedicated to
the special memory
of my youngest daughter
Jackie
1965-2008

~ CONTENTS ~

Acknowledgements

This true story has been written to the best of my knowledge, relying completely on memories which have been unlocked from my childhood thanks to the help and support of my dear wife and best friend, Joyce, who also edited the book.

Imre Istvan Koller 2009

Hungarian pronunciation

gy in *Hortobagy* or *Nagy* is like j as in juice

s in *kis* is like sh as in shower

ny in *asszony* is like ne in new

cs in *Csepel* is like ch as in chair.

Introduction

After I had first arrived in England as a refugee in 1956 I was having flashbacks of the horrors I had witnessed during the Hungarian Uprising. I used to wake up in the middle of the night in a cold sweat and suffering from stomach cramps.

At the gym where I was training there was a Chinese guru who was helping me with breathing exercises and relaxation. He was a master of Kung Fu and Yoga. He suggested to me that when I was experiencing the flashbacks it may help to think of a time when I was happy.

I followed his advice and would think back to the time I spent as a child with my two black buffalo.

As I closed my eyes I would see them come galloping towards me. *Bogar,* the larger of the two and my favourite, knelt down and as I climbed onto his back and held onto his furry neck, he grunted with pleasure.

Never, in all my young life, had I experienced love and devotion such as I felt for and received from these wonderful creatures.

The Author

Imre Istvan Koller was born in Ladánybene – a village in Bács-Kiskun county in the Southern Great Plain region of southern Hungary – on 21st June 1939.

His early childhood during the Second World War was very difficult and filled with adventure.

He spent his early years in orphanages and foster homes and did not meet his parents until 1953. He left Hungary for the first time soon afterwards to travel and work in Europe until 1956, when he became involved in the Hungarian Uprising.

In December 1956 he accepted the offer to go to England as a refugee, where he was granted British Citizenship.

In 1961 he married Joyce, a Lancashire lass, and lived near Preston for 42 years. He has a son, Steve, elder daughter Liz, younger daughter Jackie (deceased) and four grandchildren, Matt, Toby, India and Poppy.

In 2003 he returned to live in Hungary with Joyce. Now he is enjoying the fruits of his labour – drinking wine from his own vineyard, eating vegetables from his garden and living next door to his elder sister, Juci.

1. 1944 ~ My First Foster Home

The large orphanage just two and a half miles from Nagy Kôros was the first place I can remember living in. It was a large, four-storey building which housed about 800 children, 100 nuns and other staff. I do not think all that number of children were there all the time as they were fostered out to farms and houses in the area.

The upstairs rooms were dormitories, full of bunk beds. These filled both sides of the long rooms, with another row in the middle. On each floor there was a bathroom with toilets and showers but these did not always work due to the poor water pressure. More often we washed or showered outside.

The dining rooms were also very long with tables from one end to the other. Forty to fifty children used to sit at each table, with an older child serving.

Food was very scarce at that time – we were lucky to get milk with our bread for breakfast. Lunch consisted of soup and tea, perhaps bread with a little oil and paprika on it.

There was a school for the 6+ and first aid room for those who were ill. The older children went out to work during the day and returned in the evening.

I must have been five when I was told that I was going to live with an old lady. I was put on a bus and told that she would pick me up at a certain spot. She was waiting for me in a horse-drawn buggy. I remember thinking what a lovely colour the horse was – chestnut brown. She seemed very kind and introduced herself as 'Mama' – *Nagy Mama* (Grandmother) shortened to Mama or Grandma.

"Call me Mama" she said, "and I will call you Imi".

She carried on, telling me that she wanted a young boy for help and company, as she lived alone. I never found out if she had any family. I never met any.

"Have you any clothes, Imi?" she said, as I carried nothing.

"Only the clothes I am wearing", I replied.

"I will have to make you some then", she said kindly.

The clothes she made me fitted better than the ones I had.

My morning job was to tie her shoelaces, as she could not bend down that far. I found it difficult to tie them tight but with practise I managed.

After breakfast I went to the stable to feed and muck out her horse. I used to collect the eggs daily as well.

When she was cooking I stood on a chair to watch her and also helped tidy up in the house.

I can remember her always wearing a headscarf and when she smiled, she only had two front teeth, which reminded me of a rabbit.

I slept in a small bed in her bedroom and remember admiring her wardrobe, which was inlaid with brass.

One morning, when I had been living with Mama for about five months, I noticed that she was still in her bed when I awoke. She was generally up and about making breakfast. I could not stir her as I shook her. I must have realised something was the matter because I got the horse out and rode bareback to the next farm, which was over an hour away. They followed me back as quickly as they could, saying 'don't ride so fast' but I wanted to get back as quickly as possible.

The doctor was sent for. By this time it was almost dark. I was told she was dead and I would have to return to the orphanage. I remember being very upset and crying bitterly. I had been very happy living there, as she had treated me well.

Soon after staying with Mama I was fostered out to a woman who needed some help because her husband worked away in Budapest. I used to feed the animals, milk the cow and do various other jobs. I called her *Kisasszony* (little woman).

One day she said to me, 'the baby is coming'.

I looked round to see where this baby was, with my hands outstretched as if to catch it.

She took me to her bedroom and got everything ready for the birth. I was asked to put a pan of water on the stove to heat up.

I couldn't understand why she was so agitated and making funny noises.

She kept saying that the baby would not be long now.

When she eventually got on her bed and started pushing, she said she was pushing the baby out.

How can a baby get in her tummy? I thought, *and how will it get out?*

When the baby was born, it dropped onto the sheet on the bed. It looked horrible – all bloody and funny.

She told me to put it on top of her so we could cut the cord. She had some special thread which she told me to tie tight in two places.

"It won't hurt," she reassured me, then she cut it in the middle with some scissors.

I then had to wash the baby.

"Don't drop it. Make sure the water isn't too hot – put your elbow in to see."

I picked up this slippery thing and did as she told me. It was crying loudly. I thought I was hurting it. I dried and dressed it in the clothes she gave me and then I gave her the baby, which was looking a lot better than me!

"Leave me for a while," she said, "and go see to the animals and feed them."

When I returned later she had a bucket full of awful stuff (the afterbirth). She told me to dig a hole and bury it, away from the house.

She gave me a letter to take to the doctor. I had to walk for two hours to get there. The doctor asked if everything was alright and I nodded.

"I will come tomorrow morning" he said.

The next day I had to take a letter to the postman. She had written to her husband. I could see the postman's house from where she lived but it still took me a long while there and back.

Her husband returned in four weeks, saying he was not going back to work in Budapest again. He would be staying at home and I would not be needed any more. I was taken back to the orphanage, very upset again.

2. 1945 ~ The Day The Sky Turned Black

I had run away from a few foster homes after being beaten, so had returned to the orphanage again. There were nuns who looked after us; the majority were not kind but one nun in particular always used to say to me that if I was late for *ebed* (lunch) she would save me some food. I was always being told off for roaming out in the countryside. There was a large forest close by and perhaps they were afraid I would get lost.

I was always the last child in for lunch (this would save my life one day) and many times late. I loved to be outside by myself. I used to look for birds, animals, insects, flowers, anything. I took pleasure in the tranquil atmosphere away from everything. I used to lie on my back on the grass and watch the clouds roll by, making shapes out of them.

The bell had just sounded for lunch and I knew I would be late again but on this particular day something made me stop and listen. I heard a noise in the distance. This turned into a loud droning sound of engines. Gradually, as it came closer, I gasped in disbelief. The sky was dark – full of planes. There must have been at least a hundred or more flying past. On the side of each plane was a big white star on a dark background. I was told later that these were American bombers.

Suddenly, one of the planes seemed in trouble and came flying down, lower and lower. I saw the undercarriage open and bombs pour out and fall towards the ground. They fell directly on the orphanage; the impact was terrible.

The after blast sent me flying backwards and I was knocked out for a while. When I came to, I felt dizzy but gradually came round.

As I ran towards the buildings, black smoke and flames rose into the sky. There was nothing left. Everything had been flattened to the ground. It was very hot, I remember, and there was a terrible smell of burning.

Everybody inside the building was killed outright (it was lunchtime and they were all inside, having their meal). Being late had saved my life. I was the only one to survive except for a few older children who had gone out to work that day.

When I looked at the sky again, all the planes had gone.

I started running to the next village. Some people were already coming towards me. I was only very young at the time and do not remember exactly how I felt but I must have been physically and emotionally scarred by the whole experience.

I was taken to a smaller children's home on the other side of town.

Due to the chaos of War in Europe at that time, my name had been changed by one vowel. Instead of 'Koller', my name was written down as 'Kollar'. I knew nothing of my parents (in fact I had been told that I didn't have any) but I later learned that when they heard of the catastrophe at the orphanage, they were told I was dead.

The only reason I think now why I must have been placed there is because I was the oldest male child in the family with my father's name. All the children at the orphanage had no siblings with them. To evacuate a child to the countryside seemed the best thing to do. Even when I met my parents, years later when I went to Budapest, I could not ask them why I had been sent away.

3. 1946-9 ~ The Years Between

Between the age of seven and ten I had a very difficult life. I was fostered out to many farms. I had to work very hard for a young boy and was not always sent to school.

I loved school because when I was there I did not have to do any manual work. I did not mind the long walk there and back, which could be miles. I missed a lot of my schooling but when I was allowed to go, I always made up two years in one. No-one bothered if you did not attend.

Some of the boys were cruel and used to call me names because I was fostered. I was often in trouble for getting into fights I had not started. But the girls used to like me because I would stick up for them if a boy was teasing them.

When I had to work on the farm I toiled from dawn until dusk in the fields, behind the plough or looking after animals. I had to milk the cows, early morning and evening. I used to sleep in the hayloft of the barn. I loved the smell of straw and hay and was very comfortable there.

The farmers often used to take their frustration and anger out on me. If their children had misbehaved, their crops were not growing well or they had had an argument with their wife, I took the beating.

It was about this time in my life that I remember a recurring dream I used to have about how I could fly. My hair would quickly grow very long, down to my bottom. I would stretch my arms out and just fly. My hair used to get in the way across my face as I was flying and I had to push it aside. In this dream I was also able to walk through any object, walls or people. I think it was my subconscious mind helping me when I was in danger – I always escaped.

One farmer was so angry – I think his horse had trodden on his foot – that he threw a pitchfork at me, which pierced my leg.

"It's your fault, you shouldn't have got in the way!" he said. He made no effort to help me; I had to pull it out myself. It had penetrated to my shin bone and was bleeding badly. The pain was excruciating.

I ran into the barn and tore off the bottom of my shirt. I peed on it and wrapped it round my leg. It stung terribly but I knew it would disinfect the wound. I used to pee on my feet when they were sore and chapped in frosty weather. I was given boots if I went to school and, if I was lucky, when snow fell. The rest of the time I used to wrap my feet in a square of sacking, folded in a special way and tied up. In the summer it was no problem to me being barefooted.

During that night I decided to run away. Well, I couldn't run; I limped slowly and quietly. It was very painful but I was determined to get as far away from him as I could. It was nearly dawn when I reached a large forest where I thought it would be safe to hide. I spent a few weeks hiding there while my leg healed.

During the first day or two I could not do much but realised I would need shelter. I dug a hollow in the earth, covered it with branches and lined it with soft leaves. I rested and slept in there, feeling secure that no-one would find me. I ate berries, wild pears, nuts, mushrooms and hedgehogs.

I always carried a penknife and a flint in my pocket; when rubbed together they made a spark to start a fire. I would gut the hedgehog and cover it with clay. I then put it into the hot embers. When it was cooked I knocked the clay off, which had baked hard. All the prickles came away as well. The meat tasted of young piglet, which was very good, especially if you are starving. I knew which plants enhanced the flavour.

I caught rabbits and prairie dogs with a noose put round their hole. When they popped their head out, I pulled. I dried the skins and tied them together to make a poncho to keep me warm. There was enough water for me to drink from a stream but if it dried up I knew how to dig down in the earth and water would seep upwards.

When I felt I could manage to walk back to the children's home, I decided to go. I knew it would take me a few hours. It was getting cold now, at the end of October. I knew I could not survive there much longer.

As I arrived back at the home they said, "Not you again!" My leg had healed pretty well but I had left a slight hole. When I told the staff what had happened, they said that I must have deserved it.

The time I was allowed to go to school was wonderful for me. I enjoyed all the subjects, especially maths. I must have been good at that subject because the teacher always put a boy or girl next to me who needed help.

I loved animals. Anything I could call my friend. One day I found a young grass snake in the water and took it back with me. He was a greeny-brown colour and about one foot long. I gave him milk to drink and caught mice, grasshoppers and frogs, sometimes young chicks. He soon got used to me feeding him and after a few weeks he looked a lot fitter.

I kept him in a box at first. When he started to recognise me I took him with me, wrapped around my waist under my shirt. I used to take him to school and put him in a drawstring bag on my coat hook. He slept there until school finished.

In Hungary, children's school days were split up. Younger children went 8.00am to 12.00pm and older children 1.00pm-5.00pm.

One day I forgot to put my snake in the bag and left him wrapped round me. I did not realise this until my teacher's face changed as she started to stare at me. My snake had popped his head out of my shirt!

The children in the class were speechless, some girls screamed and pointed.

 "Sorry," I said to the teacher, "I forgot to take him out of my shirt!" I wasn't told off and was allowed to show him to the class. He was very tame and never hurt me but I realised that as he was growing larger I would need to find a proper home for him. But I couldn't let him go back into the wild, as he was used to being fed. The school helped me to have him rehoused in a reptile centre where he could live with other snakes.

Another time I was allowed to keep a puppy. One day the dog on the farm had some pups. I knew the farmer would get rid of them so I took one away to look after. I used to take it back to its mother for her to feed. The farmer must have realised this and asked me if I had a puppy. I told him I had; it wasn't any use lying. He must have had a good day because he let me keep him.

The pup was about 3-4 weeks old then and I loved him so much and called him Blacky. Over the next few months I trained him to herd cattle and other animals. He would come to me as soon as I whistled and was very obedient. I was heartbroken when the farmer sold him for a good price which had been offered to him.

Once I was sent to a farm approximately 60 miles away. It was very hard for me there. I had no schooling and had to work very hard all day. After I had been there a few months I felt that my neck was rather sore. Over the next week or so it got more painful until the whole of my neck was swollen and very tender. I may have been bitten by an insect or scratched at a spot which had got some bacteria inside, I never knew.

I felt very ill and mentioned this to the farmer. He just told me not to be soft and that it would get better in time. I knew that he wasn't going to help me so in the middle of the night I ran away.

I knew that I would have to walk all the way to the nearest hospital, which was 30-40 miles away.

It took me about three days to reach the town called Uj Falu. I ate what I could find along the way.

When I arrived at the hospital I managed to walk through the front doors but then I collapsed. I had contracted septicaemia and it was threatening my life. The doctors and nurses later told me that every day for weeks I had been in and out of consciousness. I can vaguely remember having drips in my arm and drainage tubes in my neck. I must have been in hospital for almost nine months because it was spring when I was discharged, looking very frail and thin.

When I was taken back to the children's home they were told to let me have plenty of rest and not to foster me for at least a couple of months.

Three weeks later I was fostered out again.

From April to September I worked on the *puszta* looking after cattle and other animals. The *puszta* or *great plain* is a large expanse of flat, open land between the river Danube and the Carpathian Mountains. It takes up more than half the area of Hungary. Cereals, vines, tobacco, hemp and flax are grown there and livestock reared.

I had some company, which was unusual but rather pleasant for me. It was near a place called Nagy Kunsag. I called the old man 'Papa' and he called me 'Son' or 'Imi' – he was very nice to me. Food was brought to us every three weeks but it didn't last long. We used to make flat bread with the flour they had brought once the bread had gone. Salami and smoked bacon was the main meat we had as it didn't go off in the heat. I used to find birds' eggs and catch prairie dogs to make our food rations last a little longer.

The hardest work we did, besides caring for the animals, was watering them. For two hours, early morning and evening, we filled the troughs with buckets of water from a sweep pole well. There was a high trough for the big animals and a lower one for the others. These troughs were about 10m long and 0.5m deep. We used to refresh/clean ourselves in the water and also threw the dogs in to clean them. One of the dogs, called Spotty, managed to jump in himself.

It used to get very hot out on the Hungarian plain where temperatures in mid-summer could reach 30°C or more. I had a lovely summer there, riding the horses bareback, learning how to make baskets out of willow and cooking over an open fire. I loved sleeping out of doors with the moon and stars as my light.

In September I was no longer needed and went back to the children's home. Papa came to say goodbye to me at the bus stop. He told me I was the best help he had ever had.

4. My Two Black Buffalo

It must have been October 1949 when I was fostered out yet again. I was 10 years old. The children's home at Nagy Koros said some people were coming to pick me up. A man, his wife and two small children came early one morning. One of the nuns had taken me to the next village to meet them.

The children sat in a small handcart, which was pulled by the man and his wife. I was handed over to them and we started walking back to the farm. The farmer seemed pleasant and his wife also.

His name was Joseph Szabo, his wife was called Rozi and their children were a boy aged about four or five and a little girl, just walking. I cannot remember their names. I was called by my nickname, Imi. I called him *Joseph bâcsi*, which means 'Joseph sir'.

We talked along the way. He was asking what I could do. He mentioned that he had plenty of animals on his farm – cows, horses, pigs, goats, chickens, geese, turkeys and two buffalo.[1] I asked him what the buffalo did.

---

[1] Water Buffalo(*bubalis bubalus*). Many tribes have invaded Hungary in the past and each brought their livestock with them, the water buffalo being one of them. This majestic creature can

"Not very much" he replied, but he wanted them to pull the plough and for any heavy work that needed doing.

When we arrived at the farm, after approximately four hours, I was shown to where I would sleep. It was the hay loft of the barn. There was a straw mattress and blankets to keep me warm. I was used to sleeping in the loft so I did not mind at all. I was allowed to eat with this family whereas generally I ate by myself in the barn at other farms.

Later, after a meal, I was curious to look at the buffalo, so I went to the stable where they lived and immediately found myself drawn to them. I stood between them, even though the farmer had said they were not very friendly, and started talking to them. I said their names: *Bogar* (black beetle) and *Kormos* (Sooty). They grunted and let me stroke them.

I would see them every day after that and we became great friends. They would do anything for me. I even taught them to kneel down for me, to make it easy to put on the yoke before ploughing.

By the time spring came we were very busy ploughing the soil and sowing seeds and vegetables – grain, sunflowers, sugar-beet, potatoes, carrots, paprika, everything.

---

be seen today on the great plain *pusztas* of Hortobagy and Bugac National Parks in Hungary.

One day on returning from the fields with Bogar and Kormos I was very tired so decided to see if I could ride back on one of the buffalo. I asked Bogar to kneel, then I jumped on his head as he lifted me up. I crawled onto his back, holding onto his funny neck whilst commanding him to stand up.

I had a welcome ride back to the farm.

My relationship with these two buffalo was magical. Every day when I got up, which would be early, between four and five, they would grunt and come towards me. They loved me, as I did them. They would have died for me. In fact, something happened later which affected me for a long time to come.

One day the farmer and I hitched up the cart, which was loaded with wood. I was to drive the buffalo to market and he was going to follow later on his horse. It took hours to get there but I arrived before him and had sold all the wood for a good price.

He was very pleased with me when he arrived and gave me half of the profits. I went to buy some fruit; I always chose fruit rather than sweets. I used to think, *why buy a small bag of sweets when you can have a large bag of apples?* We had a meal of bread and salami and set off on the journey back home. The farmer tied his horse to the cart and sat alongside me. We munched apples on the way back.

On another occasion the farmer had taken the cart and buffalo somewhere but on the way back, being an extremely hot day, they headed straight into the pond and would not budge out of the water. He rushed back to the farm for my assistance. All I had to do was whistle to them, they got out of the pond immediately and came back of their own accord.

A few miles away there was a farmer who had some racehorses. He used to brag to everyone, saying that his horses were the best and fastest in the area. He was a friend of my farmer Joseph and between the two of them they got into friendly rivalry about horses and buffalo. Each would say their animal could run faster than the other. This was the peak of the harvest season and we had been to numerous farms helping with the buffalo and threshing machines.

It was near the end of September but still very hot on this particular day. I had been chosen to ride Bogar (the largest buffalo) in a race against the other farmer's racehorse. A large number of neighbours had come to watch and betting was plentiful. The circuit had been marked out and fenced off. It was decided to race for four laps, which was about 2½ miles altogether.

My farmer knew a buffalo was fast and could stand the pace longer than a horse, although a horse would be faster at the start.

I was very excited and a little nervous, not knowing what to expect, but I knew Bogar would do anything for me. I was going to ride bareback and barefooted, as usual, so I told him to kneel down whilst I mounted him. I was ready to go as I held onto this neck, pressing my toes onto his front legs.

Then we were off!

The horse and rider shot ahead but I kept Bogar steady as he gathered up speed slowly. I did this until we reached the third lap.

"Bogar," I said, "now go!" He snorted and started to gallop forward – he was magnificent – pure muscle and power. As we gained on the horse and overtook him, everyone was clapping and cheering. We eventually reached the finishing line at least 150 yards ahead.

I was a celebrity and was carried around on the farmer's shoulders. The feeling I had that day was out of this world. That summer with the two black buffalo was the happiest and most wonderful time of my childhood.

Little did I know of the cruel blow that would fall upon me in the next few weeks.

In mid-October the farmer told me he was selling up and moving out of the area. I never asked the reason and was never told why. Every farm animal was sold, including my beloved buffalo, which went to another farm many miles away. I couldn't control my feelings and wept openly, feeling utterly devastated.

Farmer Joseph bacsi took me to back to the children's home and said he was sorry that things had turned out like this and gave me a hug. I hugged him back. Neither of us had a dry eye. I had lived at that farm for about a year, which was the longest I had stayed anywhere before.

I was soon placed elsewhere, near the Romanian border, but I could not forget my buffalo. All I did was daydream about them.

It was sometime in January 1951 and it was very cold with a lot of snow on the ground. I was out of doors working when all of a sudden something caught my eye. In the distance I saw two black dots moving over the snow. The dots became bigger and bigger and then I heard grunting.

It was Bogar and Kormos – my beautiful buffalo had come back to me!

They seemed delighted to see me and licked me, their heads nodding. I threw my arms around each of their heads in turn and embraced them, my tears of emotion falling in the snow.

The farmer had heard all the commotion and came running to see what was happening. I explained to him that the buffalo had been sold from my previous placement and taken to another farm 50-60 miles away. They must have escaped and come to find me.

The farmer decided to keep them for the time being and wait and see what happened.

A few days later the farmer who had bought the buffalo showed up. He said that soon after he had taken them home they had run away and it had taken him all this time to catch up with them. The buffalo must have gone to look for me at the previous farm and when I was not there, they carried on until they found me. The farmer had a shotgun in his hand and suddenly held it towards my buffalo.

"Don't shoot!" the other farmer said. "I will buy them off you for the same amount you paid for them."

But the farmer said 'No!' He was mad and would not listen to reason.

Then he shot my two beloved buffalo dead in front of my eyes.

I picked up a pitchfork and ran towards him, screaming that I wanted to kill him but the other farmer held me back.

I felt my whole world had ended and wept bitterly for days.

Horses were needed to drag my buffalo away with ropes and I had to help dig a big hole to bury them in. We had to use a pickaxe at first because the topsoil was frozen.

The farmer took some of the meat for his family but I would rather have starved to death than eat it.

Even now, thinking of that moment in my life brings tears to my eyes. I would never get over the feeling of losing the only beings who had loved me so much in my early childhood.

Today, as this book is being written, I vividly recall a moment which must have been locked away in my mind and the door has just opened.

Bogar was my favourite buffalo and as he lay dying on the ground I cried out, "Bogar! Bogar!" and dropped on my knees to cradle his magnificent head in my arms. My tears were falling down my cheeks and as I looked into his eyes, he was crying too. He grunted twice and then he was gone.

Was that just a childhood fantasy or was it true?

I will never really know if he was crying.

5. A New Life Begins

I couldn't concentrate after what had happened. The farmer was getting increasingly annoyed with me as I didn't work properly and couldn't control my grief.

One day he was so furious with me he grabbed a large chain that was hanging up in the barn and beat me so badly I thought he would kill me.

My back was terribly bruised and bleeding and my left hip badly bruised. He grabbed me and threw me up into the loft and told me to stay there.

I had only been at this farm for a while but made up my mind to run away again. But I would not go back to the orphanage. This was going to be the last time I was beaten. I would go to Budapest and try my fortune there.

Before I left the barn I cut a sack at the bottom and placed it over my head so it hung down like a cape. He always removed my boots to the farmhouse at night – he had heard about my previous record of running away – so I tied some sacking around my feet and took two extra sacks. It had been snowing heavily and was very cold. When I was young it would snow on and off until Easter.

When everyone was asleep and under cover of darkness, I would make my escape. I was in terrible pain but was determined to go. I could feel my leg was stiffening up and blood dripping down my back. I peed on my shirt again to disinfect my wounds which were bleeding badly. When I put it back on they smarted so much my eyes watered.

I put the sacking cape back on again – it gave me extra warmth. His store room was not locked so I helped myself to some food to keep me going, putting it into one of the sacks. I had to try to put some distance between myself and this place and vowed I would never return to the children's home again.

It must have been some time in February when I slowly and painfully limped away into the darkness. I didn't need to worry about the farmer following my footprints in the morning as the falling snow would cover them up.

It wasn't until I was quite sure that I was a safe distance from the farmer's persecution that I could rest and I collapsed on the forest floor.

Hungary is covered with forests where wild boar, deer, foxes, wolves and even bears roam, but I was never afraid of the wild animals. I had to make a shelter as it was still snowing and very cold. I made a shelter out of broken branches, bent them over and then covered them with more branches, sacking and snow. I found some leaf mulch under the trees and put it on the ground under the shelter to lie on. It took me a whole day to do this as I was hurting so much.

For a few days I stayed in the shelter and ate some of the food I had brought with me. I melted some snow so I could have a drink. When I thought it was safe and no-one would find me, I ventured out into the forest to see what I could find to eat.

I was lucky to find a dead deer frozen in the snow. With my knife I removed the skin, then freeze dried it. It took me hours to do this as the deer was frozen solid. I would use the skin, fur-side-up to lie on in my shelter and to wrap around me like a sleeping bag. I would also cover my feet with skin for added protection. The permafrost was very cold, coming up through the ground but now I would be snug.

I managed to hack off some meat to cook as well. I started a fire with some inner skins of bark from the trees – this is very soft and easy to ignite. I still had the flint I always carried in my pocket and soon made a spark with my knife. I cooked some of the deer meat over the fire on a long piece of raw green wood, which wouldn't burn quickly. It tasted very good. Now I could save some of my other provisions for a later date.

A few days later I went back to get some more meat but the deer had gone. The footprints in the snow were both small and large – foxes and wolves must have dragged it away.

Three weeks later I was feeling much better and ready to start my journey to Budapest – to my new life. I was still only 11 years old.

It had stopped snowing but snow was still deep on the ground, getting very cold at night. I kept to the countryside and did not use the road, only occasionally looking for road signs to make sure I was going in the right direction. Now I was able to travel for longer, using the sun and stars as my guide. I didn't have a watch or a compass.

As I travelled I found corn, still on the cob, which had been left in the fields, and wild pears. These pears fall down on the ground and ripen under leaves or snow. I also ate acorns and any berries I could find.

I think it must have taken me about five weeks before I reached Budapest. I was always wary of people looking for me and didn't risk talking to anyone. I couldn't see my back, which was still very painful but my hip was getting better although still very red. I was lucky to have quick-healing skin.

Although the scars were mending outwardly, the scars inside me would take a long time to heal.

I could make out a railway line through the snow so I followed it for a few miles. There was a station ahead with a few benches along the platform. I remember the name – Kellett railway station. There was nobody around and, as I was so exhausted, I thought I would rest on one of the benches. I soon fell asleep.

I was awoken by someone shaking me and looked up into the face of a policeman. I jumped up and started to run away but he had a colleague with him who was ready to catch me. I struggled but eventually realised they were not going to hurt me.

I must have looked terrible and they stared at me in amazement. I was smelly, filthy and wearing what were now just rags, as the sacking was breaking up. I had changed my so-called footwear a number of times and had been glad of the deerskin, which was warm and strong.

"Who are you and where have you come from?" they asked.

I wouldn't tell them as I was afraid they would take me back.

"Are you hungry?" they asked.

I nodded.

They took me to the police station and gave me some food, which I devoured in a couple of minutes. Afterwards they took me along a corridor to a room where a friendly-looking woman was waiting. She looked enormous to me – as broad as she was tall. She introduced herself as Marika and told me I would need to have a shower and change my clothes.

When I was asked to take my clothes off I said, "I cannot. My shirt is stuck to my back." When I turned around I heard her gasp as she saw the dried blood on my shirt, which had completely adhered to my back.

She called the other officers in to show them. I remember them taking photographs of me when I first arrived and during the process of what they saw. Gently and slowly Marika started washing me under the shower and gradually the shirt peeled off my back. What was revealed underneath I could not see but she cried out, with tears in her eyes.

"Who has done this to you?"

Evidently my back was marked where the chain had dug deep. The skin was healing but was full of wheals which were a fiery red colour.

"My poor boy," she said, and called again to the officers. They were concerned for me and once again asked who had done this and where I had come from.

As soon as I realised they would not send me back (they told me faithfully they wouldn't), I told them my story. They could hardly believe their ears at how a young boy could survive all that. I must have walked at least 150 miles and with the injuries I had, combined with not much food and freezing temperatures, it seemed a miracle I had made it.

An ambulance came and took me to hospital, where I had an operation on my back to smooth out the skin. I was told that all the scars would vanish in time. I was there for about three weeks.

Marika came to visit me, as well as the two police officers. They were very kind to me and brought me presents, clothes, sweets and books. I think Marika was a social worker, for it was she who took me to the children's home in Budapest.

I never found out if the farmer who inflicted my wounds was brought to justice.

6. Budapest

I soon settled down to my new life and was very happy at the home in Budapest. I was sent to school and given a test to see how far I had got with my grades. I would have to work very hard to make up for two years in one. I did this for two years – doing four years work in two. I had passed all my grades when I left school, aged 14. In the new school year I would have to go for higher education.

I needed to keep busy; being busy was the only life I knew. I had seen a bicycle in a shop window that I wanted. It was yellow and white with chrome mudguards. They allowed me to apply for a job in a baker's shop as errand and delivery boy. I was 12 years old then. No-one bothered about the age of a child who worked in those days. The job had an early start from 6.00am to 12.00 noon. I attended school from 1.00pm-5.00pm so that fitted in very nicely for me.

I delivered bread and cakes to other shops using the bicycle they supplied me with – it had a basket on the front. When they found out I came from a children's home they gave me the off-cuts from the cakes to take back for all the children.

It took me many months to save up for my racing bike. My boss asked me why I was working so hard, as

I had never missed a day. I told him I was saving up for a special bike which I had seen. It cost 400 forint which was equivalent to £150 then. I received 20 forint every week from my job – I also used to move snow from pavements in the winter after school to make more money. I didn't save it all; I liked to spend some as well.

One day my boss asked me how much more I had to save before I could buy the bike. It might have been about 50 forint.

"Come on," he said. "I am coming with you to buy it."

All the staff at the bakery had collected the money for me and I was told I was the best young worker they had ever had. The boss came with me to the shop and haggled with the owner about the price. I got the bike at a cheaper price and had money left over for a toolkit and carrier bag. I couldn't thank them enough and was so proud of my new bike which was cleaned and polished regularly and looked after well. It was my pride and joy.

I was having problems with a boy one year older than me at school, who kept on bullying me, telling me I had no parents and that I was a bastard. One day I could not stand it any more. It was like waving a red rag to a bull. I bent down and rushed head forwards towards him, knocking him down and winding him. Then I jumped on top of him, fists flailing.

This photograph was taken after I had been living in England for about year. I was training hard for my boxing and as you can see am still wearing my special badge of honour on my lapel.

This is the only family photograph I have of my parents and siblings, taken just after I met them in 1953. I am on the back row between my sisters Juci and Erzsi.

Imre and wife Joyce at their home in Hajos.

Imre enjoying a glass of wine outside his *pince* (wine cellar).

All of a sudden, strong hands grabbed my collar and my tormentor's also and we were parted.

It was the sports master.

"If you want to fight you must do it properly," he said, and took us to the gym, where there was a boxing ring. We were given boxing gloves and told to carry on our argument in the ring.

I don't think we had been fighting for more than two minutes before the bully he had had enough and ran out of the ring. The sports master was very impressed with me and asked if I would like to train for amateur school boxing. He weighed me. At that time I was eating like a horse and putting on weight. I had to put on a couple of kilos, then I could fight bantam weight.

After that initial fight with my tormentor I immediately gained respect from my peers. No-one dared bully me again. I had six weeks training, at which I excelled; my only problem was that I could not skip. I was told I had two left feet!

My first match was for the Hungarian Schools Championship. I was told by my trainer just before the fight to be careful, as my opponent was very good. Amateur boxing at that time consisted of three, two-minute rounds.

Although he was a year older than me, I wasn't really worried. Early on, he hit me hard on the nose, which hurt and made me mad. I went for him and towards the end of the first round I hit him so hard that he fell flat on his back. At the end of the round my trainer jumped into the ring so fast. He told me he had never seen anyone's hands move as fast as mine.

When I received my award for winning the championship I walked up to be presented with a silver cup and a medal. All the staff and children were present, as well as teachers and children from the school.

I got a standing ovation as I was handed my silver cup. As I held up the trophy and faced the audience I shouted and jumped for joy. I held the cup over my head and walked back to my seat. Everyone was patting me on the back and saying 'well done'.

I felt wonderful, like I had been re-born. I had respect from everybody.

Life had changed so much for me in the past year – from rags to riches – for life was now so rich for me.

Rich in hope.

7. I Find My Parents

One day, an old lady came to the home where I lived. She wanted to give a good home to a child who had no parents. At the time I was nearby, playing with some other children.

When she saw me she said "I want *that* boy" and pointed at me. She was told she could have a girl but she said she had other lodgers who were all men and a girl wouldn't be suitable. I thought perhaps she would choose another boy but she was adamant she wanted me.

I wondered why she wanted me and not one of the others. I asked her later and she replied, "Because you looked like you needed some love."

She had a feeling for me; she felt I was different.

It put an idea in my head which was quite exciting. If I went to live with her I would feel more independent and wouldn't have to live in the children's home.

The more I thought about it the more I wanted to do it. At first the principal said 'no' I couldn't go, but I pestered and pestered until eventually he gave in to me.

I moved into Elizabeth Duda's house in December 1952. I was 13½ years old. She lived in Csepel, a borough of Budapest. There were five lodgers living there and I shared a room with three of them. She washed and cooked for everyone and even took a midday meal to the factory where the men worked.

Whilst I lived there I carried on with my schooling. I had to catch a bus, as the house was further away. When I left the children's home I left my bike there so that the other children could use it.

Everyone called Elizabeth Duda 'Little Mama'. She was small and slim but her most important feature was her hair. It was so long it reached the ground and was white as snow. Every morning she used to sit in the garden, winter or summer, on a seat that was curved around the trunk of a tree. She would brush her hair, then roll it round and round into a bun on top of her head.

I was fascinated by watching her do this and recall it vividly. Nobody knew how old she was but one of the lodgers, who had lived there for many years, said she still looked the same as she did then.

She had a private room which she kept locked and were not allowed inside. We always wanted to know what went on in her private room but never really got the chance to find out.

Mama was also a healer/fortune-teller and people came to see her from all over to have their fortunes told, even from other countries.

On one occasion there was a big commotion when some people came over from America. They were FBI agents and must have heard about Mama. Two children had been kidnapped for ransom and had been missing for about two weeks. They were brother and sister. The agents brought clothing which belonged to them.

Mama held the clothing for a few minutes and then told them she had some very bad news. She took them and an interpreter into her private room. They kept on going in and out of the house to their car, which had tinted windows. I think they had some kind of radio telephone in there.

After many calls to America and back we later found out that she had directed the police to a sewer where both children were found, naked and dead. She also told the authorities where the kidnappers (murderers) lived. They immediately went to arrest them. They lived only four miles from where the bodies had been found.

On another occasion Mama spoke to a neighbour whose husband had been missing, presumed dead or imprisoned, since the Second World War. Mama told her that he would return on a certain day – the 3rd of

July 1951. She made this prediction in 1948. Sure enough, this miracle happened, exactly as she had prophesied.

I lived with Mama for about eight months and during that time she healed people who couldn't walk before seeing her but who walked away afterwards. I was very happy during that period of my life and enjoyed living there. She always wanted to tell my fortune but I wouldn't let her.

The lodgers who lived there always left their newspapers on the table when they had finished reading them and I used to have a look through them. I had begun to wonder about my parents and would look for lists or notices of families with missing children. I was doing this one day when my eyes focussed on the name 'Koller', which sounded strangely like my own – 'Kollar'. I cannot remember why their name was in the paper but decided to contact them. They lived in Kiralyedo – a village 15 miles from Budapest.

It took me a few times to pluck up courage, for when I arrived at the house I saw several children coming and going. On about the third attempt I went straight up to the door and knocked.

A lady answered and asked what I wanted.

I said I was a student doing a project on children during the war of 1939-45. She asked me inside and made a drink.

I asked if she had lost any of her family.

She replied 'yes' she had. A boy who was born in 1939.

His name was Imre Koller.

She said that he had been killed at an orphanage at Nagy Koros in 1945.

The hairs on the back of my neck stood on end and I went hot all over but I couldn't say what I had planned, so I just asked if I could come back on Saturday and talk some more.

It was arranged that this is what I would do.

I arrived on time, having rehearsed in my mind what I wanted to say. A man was also there this time and the children were shoved out into the garden.

I sat at the table, looking across at them both.

"I have something to tell you," I began. "I think I am your lost son."

My mother jumped up and flung her arms around me.

"I knew when I first saw you!" she exclaimed.

The man, my father, got up and embraced me.

My parents had gone to Nagy Koros to bring me home after the war but were told that all the children in the orphanage had been killed. The only ones who survived were older children who had gone to work. The records didn't state that only I had survived out of the younger ones.

The rest of the family were called in and I was introduced to my brothers and sisters – four boys and four girls. It was a very emotional meeting with many tears of joy. I could now say that I had a father and mother.

I stayed for a meal but didn't want to sleep there.

I visited them only about six times and used to walk along and talk to three of my sisters – Juci, Erzsi and Kati – but we didn't get very close. I didn't have very much in common with them at that time.

I told my parents about my boxing and that soon I would be going on tour with the club. They didn't seem very keen about me doing that, saying I was too young and that I might get hurt. Little did they know about my past life – I never told them – but I felt stifled. There was no way I was to give up my boxing.

I could sense that there were problems ahead and was glad I was going away for a few months.

Over the next three and a half months I was entered into the European Schools Boxing Championship – visiting Italy, Switzerland, France, Germany and England. After that came the International Schools Championship and we travelled to Russia, China and America.

I won all my matches but one and was presented with a special badge of honour. It was shaped like the Hungarian royal crown and made of 24ct gold. Only a few of these badges had been made and were given to deserving people who had achieved a lot in a short period of time. I wore mine with pride, on the lapel of my jacket. Years later it was stolen by a so-called friend. I never saw him afterwards.

I had to carry on with my school studies whilst I was away and had a tutor. I was the youngest in the group and was aged about 14.

Whilst I was away I was thinking about what my parents would say when I returned. I knew they wanted me to go and live with them and most certainly would want to stop me boxing. I began to feel very uncertain about everything and felt suffocated.

On one of my visits to my parents' house I met my grandmother Koller. There was instant spark between us and we got on very well. She asked me if I would like to go on a bicycle ride to Ladanybene, where she lived and where I had been born.

I agreed and I think we rode there three or four times over the next few weeks. It took us at least three hours to get there. She was very fit and never seemed to get tired. She used to chew tobacco and drink a litre of wine every day.

She showed me the house, which had been taken from my parents by the Communists. It was now occupied by some big-head Russian officer. It was a large farmhouse with stables adjoining and over 2,000 hectares of land.

The property was situated in a small village called Tatarszentgyorgy. Tenant farmers had lived in small cottages on the land and helped my father with the crops, grapes, etc. There was a lot of livestock, including horses, cattle, pigs and chickens.

She told me that my mother was a very good pianist and used to have a grand piano with glass legs.

After the communists took over, anyone who had a large property with more than two hectares of land was classed as *bourgeois* (a middle class citizen).

My family were thrown out of their house and rehoused two miles away in a small hovel. My father was never the same man afterwards. He took to drinking a lot.

I built up a good relationship with my grandmother, better than with my parents, so I went to see her more often than them, even though it meant a long bicycle ride there and back.

Although I didn't know her for long, she became a very special person in my life at that time.

The last time I saw my grandmother I knew I wouldn't see her again because I had made up my mind to leave Hungary and go to Austria. I cried nearly all the way back to Csepel.

Two days later when I left Mama's early in the morning, as I usually did when I went training at the gym, I said goodbye to her. She never said a word; I think she just knew. I had my boxing kit in my bag along with all the money I had been saving. I hadn't told anyone I was leaving. I knew my parents would try to stop me. I didn't use public transport but walked, following the railway track. I knew that it was the line to Austria.

After a while I threw my boxing kit away to make room for some provisions for my journey, which I had bought from a shop. It was August 1953. I had turned

14 in June. The boxing training had made me very fit and I had grown taller and put on weight. I was not a skinny little urchin any more.

It took me three weeks to get to the Austrian border.

8. Austria

I had a pretty uneventful journey along the way. The weather was good and when my food ran out there was fruit and vegetables in the fields. One day a delicious aroma filled my nostrils. I had stumbled upon an outdoor cooking oven, which was close to a farmhouse. I crept closer and had a look inside. There were rows of large, round loaves of bread.

My mouth was watering as I hadn't eaten properly for a while but the bread was not cooked yet. I would have to wait until it was ready. After 45 minutes or so I leaned forward, opened the door and with the wooden paddle I had found, I scooped out my prize.

A shout made me jump and I turned to see an angry farmer's wife running towards me. I ran for dear life, as fast as I could, juggling the scorching hot loaf from hand to hand. When I had run a good distance I took out my knife and cut a large chunk from it. It was so delicious! I kept on eating until I was full. The next two days I was ill because I had eaten too much hot, new-baked bread.

Whilst I had been at Mama's house, one of her lodgers used to tell me about the time he was a border guard at the Hungarian/Austrian border. I had listened to his story with interest but at the time I had no idea just how useful to me all the information it provided was going to be.

I was getting close to the border now and feeling very excited but fearful of what might happen. There were four stages to get through, I had been told. Guards in look-out towers every mile, and guards patrolling every 30 minutes.

I put down my bag and hid it beneath a bush, then walked slowly and quietly to check how close I was.

I nearly walked into two guards who were talking to each other. I could have almost touched them. I dropped quickly to my knees and hid myself in some undergrowth. I hadn't realised I was so close to the Border. Luckily they didn't see me and walked away.

Beads of perspiration were running down my face as I moved back 150 yards and waited and checked the times of the patrol. The area where I hid had good shrub cover; no-one would see me. It took me two days to pluck up courage to go but when I made up my mind, nothing would stop me – except perhaps a bullet.

I got to the first stage and all was clear. It was 20 yards wide and criss-crossed with tripwires which, if touched, would set off rockets. The weeds and grass were high between the wires and I was very careful when stepping in between them.

By the time I reached the second stage I was wet with sweat already. My mouth was dry with fear, so I had a quick drink of water.

The second stage was No-Man's Land – 50 yards of nothing. I crawled on my stomach and picked up a big clump of tumbleweed which had blown next to me, dragging it behind me. I tied it to my leg, leaving my hands free. This gave me good camouflage.

The guards had returned again. They set off two by two, met in the middle, crossed over, and then walked back to the look-out tower. My heart was beating so fast and loud I thought they might hear it. I heard them talking as I lay beneath the weed. I was lucky the grass was long and uncut but I had to be careful in order not to leave a trail behind me.

"Look at all that tumbleweed!" one of them said. "We must tidy it away later, it's blocking our view."

Quite a lot of weed was blowing about. It is very light and clumps can reach as much as three feet in circumference. I waited until they had crossed over and were heading back.

The third stage, which was the worst, was the minefield, 10 yards wide, laid out like chessboard squares under the soil. I had to poke gingerly with my knife and when I found a mine, I had to judge carefully the distance to the next.

I found at least 20 mines and put a small marker next to them. I was crouching on my knees in the minefield, which was also deep with grass. I think adrenaline took over and got me through safely.

I had chosen this time of year because I knew that all the vegetation would be tall and that the guards wouldn't see me through the greenery. I still had the tumbleweed with me which was very light and didn't hamper me.

My heart was thumping and the hairs were standing up on my neck. I had no second chance. If I made a mistake, that was it.

The fourth stage was five yards of barbed wire.

On my stomach again I dug underneath the wire with my knife until it was big enough for me to squeeze beneath. I left the tumbleweed in the hollow I had made in the ground to disguise it.

I still had to be extremely careful but I couldn't see any guards patrolling close by, so as fast as I could I crawled along until I reached the safety of a cornfield, which was high with corn.

Not until I was in the middle of the field did I start running. I didn't stop until I collapsed through sheer exhaustion and fear.

When I opened my eyes I saw a man standing over me. I lashed out with my knife but luckily didn't touch him. I think he must have carried me to his house as I don't remember walking there. I came round in his kitchen with my knife still firmly grasped in my hand.

"You are in Austria now, my son," he told me.

After a good meal and rest that night he told me that he would have to inform the authorities that I had come across the border from Hungary. Two border police officers came and were astounded at what I had done. They said I was the youngest person they had known to cross the border uninjured. Only one in a thousand made it alive and I was one of them.

They took me to their headquarters and listened to my statement. They took my photograph and fingerprints so that they could sort out my work permit. I would be able to stay and work in Austria for two years. The permit was also valid for West Germany.

I stayed a few more days with the farmer and helped him out on his farm. He asked me if I wanted to see how far I had run that day. He took me in a horse and cart to near the border. I couldn't believe that I could have run so far without stopping; it took just over an hour to get there.

I moved to Imstyrol and started looking for a job. It wasn't long before I found work with a logging company. I did a man's work and received a man's wage. They didn't bother what age I was. I used to help fell trees after the top had been lopped.

It wasn't long before I was promoted to lopper. The man whose job it was before me had been stupid. He had been provided with a safety harness and hat but never wore them. One day he fell and was badly injured. He was taken to hospital but never recovered.

No-one else wanted the job but I said "If you pay me the same wage as he got, I will do it." I was fearless and would try anything. I got the job. I wasn't afraid of heights but was always careful and wore the safety equipment, along with crampons clipped onto my shoes, making it easy to grip the tree.

I worked with the logging company for six months until the work was over for that season. I was told that if I came that way next Autumn I would have a job waiting for me.

I decided to leave Austria and caught a train to West Berlin. I'd purchased a student rail card that would enable to me to travel anywhere in Europe except behind the Iron Curtain. There was no Berlin Wall between East and West then, only a large wire fence with border guards every 30 yards or so. They all carried Kalashnikov machine guns.

Because I had some time on my hands, I took a job as a street cleaner to conserve my savings. I only did that for two weeks, then carried on with my travels. Over the next two years I visited many countries. When my money was running short I used to work for a while to top it up.

9.   1956 ~ The Uprising

In September 1956 I was back in Germany and working in Stuttgart. For the last few months I had been making high-pressure hosepipes in a rubber factory. Some of the workers were talking about an advertisement in one of the newspapers. Evidently something was brewing up politically in Hungary. They were looking for men who spoke the language fluently and knew Budapest very well.

"Why don't you go and see what it's all about?" my workmates urged me. I would have to get to West Berlin in two days for the interview.

I decided to try my luck, not knowing what the job consisted of. The manager gave me some German marks, which had been collected from the men. He wished me every success and said there was always a job waiting for me if not.

At the interview I was initially asked my age. I lied and said I was 20, which was the youngest they would accept. In fact I was only 17. The job consisted of getting into Hungary by parachute, taking films and recording the events that were happening, then getting the films back to Austria. Fifteen men applied for eight jobs and I was accepted as № 8.

Although they were sceptical about my age they didn't look at my work permit and gave me the job because I spoke fluent Hungarian and knew Budapest so well.

Five days of intensive training then began – learning to handle cine cameras, photo cameras, tape recorders and parachute jumping. We started the day with physical training for two hours, then went to the classroom for camera practice. The afternoon was parachute training, jumping from a high platform with a special harness. More physical training in the evening. I excelled at everything and felt elated. I got on well with the other seven men, who were called 1-7; we had no names, only numbers.

On the 19th of October we were told to prepare to fly and be dropped by parachute close to Budapest. We wore dark clothing and carried our kit (cameras, films and recorders) to the plane. We were not given a gun and were advised not to accept one. I never used a gun all the time I was there – the only shooting I did was with a camera. We had no papers and had to remember everything in our heads. We were told that when we reached Budapest we must split up. We each had a different part of the city to go to.

It was dark when were told to jump out of the plane. I enjoyed it and took everything in my stride. I had been chosen to whistle to everyone once on the ground as I could whistle with my tongue, which was the shrillest. Everyone landed safely and we gathered together. All the parachutes were hidden deep in the middle of some bushes, hoping they wouldn't be found. We then waited for our equipment, which was parachuted separately, and then carried it on our backs in rucksacks.

We each had our own assignment clear in our heads. As we parted we shook hands and went our separate ways. We would meet up at a designated place in five days' time.

The first few days were peaceful. There were many demonstrations going on and people of all ages were involved. Russian tanks and soldiers were about but stayed out of the way. On 23rd October there were two groups of demonstrators – 200,000 students and citizens – one group walking to the Hungarian radio station to have their demands read on air, the other to the Parliament building, where I was filming.

It was the AVO Hungarian Secret Police,[2] who were much hated and feared, who initially opened fire into these crowds of peaceful demonstrators. Russian troops and tanks followed. In less than a minute 200 people lay dead. That was the catalyst that triggered the Uprising. Russia was squeezing the life blood out of Hungary, cutting down forests for timber, taking

---

[2] The AVO Secret Police were conceived as an external appendage of the Soviet Union's secret police forces from 1945-1956.

grain, corn, vegetables and fruit, everything. Food was getting very scarce. People were forced out of their homes if they owned more than two hectares of land (as my parents had) and had to share a home with others. Sometimes three families lived in one house.

I do not know why it was me who was chosen to take the negatives back to Austria but on 24th October we all met up and they all handed them over. I was given a 2-stroke Hungarian-made Paojna motorbike, together with details of how to get to the border. It took me two and a half hours to get there and meet my connection in Austria. By that time the borders were now open, the minefields dismantled, so I rode through with no problems. I handed over the negatives and was given new films for our future use in exchange.

When I arrived back in Budapest we regrouped, only to learn that two of our group had been shot. There were now only six of us left.

The next few days were very bad. I do not want to talk about it too much as it was very distressing for me. There were tanks and guns firing, people shouting and screaming, dead bodies lying in the street.

I was there taking shots on that particular day, the 25th October 1956, outside the government house at the rear of the Parliament building. An hour later firing was heard and people scattered as Russian tanks approached. I made a quick exit as the shooting started.

Later on that day (I will never forget it as long as I live) I was taking some still shots with my camera when I felt something push into my back. I turned and looked into the barrel of a Kalashnikov machine gun in the hands of a Russian soldier. Five others were with him and I was told to put up my hands whilst they searched me. All I had was my camera.

They marched me along to where a tank and a troop carrier were standing. Their commanding officer was there. He was talking very fast and shouting at me. I couldn't understand Russian so I didn't know what he was saying.

They pushed me towards the Danube so my back was towards it. There was a high wall there and they were standing with their backs to it. The officer was pointing a revolver at me and shouting.

"This is it, the end is coming," I thought.

Then, all of a sudden, I saw some heads appear from behind the wall. It was a band of freedom fighters. In less than a minute all the Russians were lying dead on the ground. My knees were like jelly and I shook all over, sobbing like a baby. They came and embraced me and told me I had been great. They took the tank and I went with the others in the troop carrier. It wasn't safe to hang around there for long.

We were quite close to my safe house so I asked them to stop for me to get out. I thanked them again for saving my life. I never saw them again. They drove away, waving.

On 26th October I met another band of freedom fighters who I knew. They told me that some more of my group had died. They didn't know who or how many. They handed over the negatives that had been given to them and I made my way to Austria again.

This time I took the country back-roads as I had heard that there were a lot of tank convoys further up the main road. The border was still clear as I crossed.

When I arrived back in Budapest again no-one came to our meeting point. I realised that I must be the only one left. It hit me very hard. At one time I felt like giving up.

On the evening of 26th October I met some more freedom fighters who were talking about a radio message they had received from the Buda area, asking for help. They were going some time before daylight so I told them I would join them and took my cine camera with me.

The only problem was that no-one knew how to drive the tank they had found. I mentioned that I had driven a caterpillar tractor before. There was not much difference, I thought. It *was* quite different, as I found out, especially the controls, but I managed to cope after a few hundred yards.

We crossed the Danube over the Freedom Bridge (as it is now called). It was then called Franz Joseph bridge. Gunfire whistled over our heads. Quickly I drove by the side of the Gellert Hotel and up the hill to the Fisherman's Bastian.[3]

I had stopped just as we drove over the bridge to let some men off the tank. These, with others, went to surround the Russians from the rear and after a wait of five minutes to let them get into place, we carried on to the front. We had been told there were some traitors from the Hungarian Secret Police with the Russians.

Once they opened fire we retaliated and exchanged fire for about two hours. I couldn't film at this time and just crouched down inside the tank, listening to the noise of the bullets.

When everything went quiet I got out to film. There was carnage everywhere. We turned a corner and what met our eyes was unbelievable. I saw hell that

---

[3] The Fisherman's Bastian, built in 1905, is a terrace in neo-gothic and neo-Romanesque style on the Buda bank of the Danube. There are seven towers and from these offer panoramic views of the area.

day – people of all ages – men, women and children – hung up onto trees, railings, everything. As I was filming this, I was crying. I saw grown men on their knees sobbing.

As morning came, wagons arrived to take the dead bodies away. I don't know where they took them. As we headed back to the bridge, it was now the 27th October, we had a few more skirmishes but reached Pest all in one piece. We were all crying. I felt like my heart was breaking and couldn't get the picture out of my head of all those innocent people hanging there.

After the first Russian offensive had been quashed and their soldiers had surrendered or been taken prisoner, it went quiet for a few days.

Word went around that the freedom fighters who had commandeered Russian tanks and armoured vehicles were listening in to the Russians on their two-way radios. They heard Russian soldiers talking and some of the men could understand the language. These newly-drafted troops were talking about Suez. The Suez crisis was happening in Egypt at the same time. The Soviet Prime Minister, Bulgarin, had made it clear that Russia would take action against any aggression in Egypt.

One of the freedom fighters spoke to one of the Russians over the radio, saying "Where do you think you are?"

They answered "Suez Canal."

"You are not. You are in Budapest," he replied. "You are on the other side of the Danube in Buda and we are in Pest."

Suddenly it went very quiet as their commanding officer shouted at them to turn the thing off. After that the Russians jammed all the radio wavelengths.

We couldn't believe what they had said. Surely they hadn't been brainwashed into thinking they had gone to the Suez Canal? Hungary would definitely be much colder than Egypt. We never found out any more.

On 29th October I had been asked to go and see Imre Nagy, who was the Prime Minister for Hungary during the uprising. He had heard that I was the only film recorder left out of eight and wanted to tell the people something. Some of the freedom fighters thought it was a trap. I told them that if I didn't come back, to go and blow the place up.

I shook hands with Imre Nagy and he praised me for my bravery. He didn't realise I was so young. He spoke personally to me, saying he never really wanted the job but the people wanted and needed him. He also said that he knew when the second offensive came, if he was captured he would be hanged.

As I was leaving we shook hands and embraced each other.

"Why don't you come with me?" I said to him. "You will be safe."

"I cannot," he smiled and replied, "Hungary needs me."

On 16th June 1958 Imre Nagy was hanged. He was the martyred hero of the 1956 Uprising of the Hungarian people against the Russian oppressors. In 1989 there was an emotional reburial of Imre Nagy and his associates in the Kozma Street cemetery, where they had been hastily thrown after their executions.

Until 5th November it was relatively peaceful. All the streets had been cleared of bodies and debris from the first offensive. Luckily at this time it was very cold, with freezing temperatures. With the second offensive the Russians came with all their might. Tanks and troops came across all the bridges of the Danube – they were everywhere.

The fighting lasted for five very intense days. In the end the freedom fighters had to surrender as they had run out of ammunition and petrol. The Russians first took over Buda and then moved into Pest. I was moved all over the city to make sure I wasn't caught.

As time went by, many people were rounded up and shot or put in prison.

From 10th November to 12th December I was playing hide-and-seek with the Russians and taking more films in between. I had a few close encounters but luck was still on my side. I used the cellars to get around – Budapest has a labyrinth of cellars – and as the majority of the partition walls had been broken down, it was easy to go for miles without being seen.

But I realised that soon I would need to get away. It was becoming very dangerous. I would have to get to Austria again before I was caught. My gear and all the films were hidden in a special cellar near the bus depot, which I was thinking would be my place of departure.

10. Freedom

On 13th December 1956 I decided to go to see Little Mama one more time before I left Hungary. I realised that it would probably be the last time I saw her. I did think of going to see my parents as well but they lived further away and I didn't have time. It would be too dangerous for me to go that far. I also knew they would try to stop me from going.

I went at about 10.30am and as I was walking along her street I saw an old woman about 300 yards in front of me. All of a sudden she stopped and spun round. She stared at me, then raised her arms into the air and came towards me. I ran towards her as fast as I could until we met and hugged each other. I picked her up and whirled her round and round.

"Put me down, put me down Imi!" she said, as she hung onto me. "I will get dizzy!" It was an emotional moment for us both as I had been away for three years. She said that I had grown and broadened out in that time but that she would have recognised me even if I had been in a crowd of a thousand people.

Walking back to her house she told me the bad news of Sandor, her eldest lodger. He had died. She said she was heartbroken as she had tried to save him with her powers but could not. I used to call him Papa and play chess with him. Mama gave me a gold watch he had left me but I told her to keep it, or sell it and give the money to charity. I asked her how she knew I was behind her in the street.

"I had a feeling you were there," she replied.

I stayed with her for over an hour. We talked and had a meal. As she left the room to make me a sandwich for later, one of the other lodgers said that she had told them "Imi is back – he will come to see me."

I stood up and said I'd have to leave before the curfew at 7.00pm. It was a long walk back to Budapest. I kissed her on both cheeks and said goodbye. She kissed me back. I didn't say what I was going to do and she didn't ask but I knew she would have some idea. The men gave me some forints to help me out as I hadn't much money left. I said goodbye again and left.

I walked back with no problems that evening, thinking about how to get a vehicle that I could drive to Austria with all my cameras and negative films. On 14th December I was walking around taking pictures and trying to pluck up courage to go to the bus depot. People were being arrested all over the city, so I went back to my house via the cellars.

At midnight I made up my mind to go across the road to where the bus depot was. I thought it as good a day to die as any. I had to cross a wide road to get there, so when I felt it was safe, I ran quickly to the other side.

Once I was inside the depot a man shouted, "Hey you! We're closed until 5 o'clock."

"Can we talk somewhere safe?" I asked him, and we shook hands.

"Come with me," he said.

I followed him into a dining room. Six other men were there. They had been servicing the buses, getting them ready for the morning shift.

"Promise not to do anything stupid towards me," I said. "I am a reporter from the Uprising and need your help to get all my equipment and films back to Austria safely."

His eyes nearly jumped out of his sockets.

One of the men stepped forward, dropped on his knees and said, "I have heard about you but didn't think I would ever meet you." He shook my hand. Everybody started crying and we cried together for about 10 minutes until someone said, "We can't go on like this – we have a lot of work to do for this young man." They told me to return that same day, the 15th December, in the late evening when everything would be ready.

I returned that evening as arranged and they showed me my bus and the alterations that had been done. They had reinforced the front and sides with steel plates fitted inside the bus. There was more steel reinforcement further down, under the front window, with two holes for me to look through. This had been done in case I was fired on directly, so I could duck down, look through the holes and carry on driving.

They explained about the gears and said there was a full tank of petrol. They also gave me a driver's uniform which I had to wear. Everyone laughed when they showed me the dummy they had made, dressed up as a conductor (all buses had a conductor then).

"If you get a passenger who is willing to dress up as her, that will be better," they said.

It was fixed for a 5.00 am start from the bus depot on the 16th December. They had put a destination on the front as if it was a bus picking up passengers along the way. I put on my uniform and peaked cap, said goodbye to them and thanked them for all their help.

"One more thing before you go," they said.

One of the men drew a small black moustache across the top of my lip.

"Now you look more like the part and not so young," he said

I had a quick look in the mirror and it certainly looked real. I pulled my cap down over my face and felt that no-one would recognise me. They all had tears in their eyes when I left with the conductor dummy on the back seat.

As I drove through the streets towards the Danube I knew there would be a road block over the bridge. When I got to the centre of Franz Joseph bridge I saw some Russian soldiers stopping trucks and cars ahead of me. As I got closer they saw a bus being driven normally so they waved me on. I saluted them as I passed by and one soldier saluted back. It was so easy and I couldn't believe I had got through so quickly. I had kept very calm and in control of my nerves, so nothing looked unusual about me.

I had to stop or slow down at every bus stop along the way, just in case there were any passengers. I passed through Buda and into the countryside, where I saw someone walking. I stopped and asked him if he wanted a lift.

"I'm going to Austria," he said.

"I am too," was my reply, "come on then."

He was walking rather oddly as he climbed up the steps onto the bus. He wore a long top coat which was bulging strangely.

As he got closer to me he said, "You are very young for a bus driver."

I laughed at him, then asked what was under his coat. He opened it and there was a Kalashnikov machine gun and a belt full of grenades.

"You've come well prepared!" I said.

"They will not catch me alive," he replied.

I started off again and drove a few more miles. We stopped when we saw a group of people walking at the side of the road.

"Where are you going?" one of them shouted.

"We're going to Austria. Come on, we'll take you."

Three men and one woman got onto the bus. I asked the woman if she would dress up in the conductress's uniform and throw the dummy away. She stripped down to her underclothes and said, "Have a good look – that's the last time you'll see me like this!" Everyone laughed.

Going along, I picked up more people until the bus was full of men, women and four children. I knew the route very well so as we reached the last bend before the border, which was approximately two miles away, I stopped the bus. I told everyone we were close to the border and if anyone wanted get out and try their luck alone, they could. Nobody moved.

It was now or never as we set off again.

As we drove long I told them all to get down in a safe place. All the men started opening windows. Some didn't open so they started smashing them with the butts of their guns. I told them to do it quietly in case the border guards heard. They put their coats against the glass to muffle the noise.

All were ready, with guns poised, as I set off on the most hair-raising journey of my life. My foot was right down on the throttle.

As we got closer the Russian border guards were standing across the road in a line, firing. Everyone on the bus started firing back – the noise was deafening.

My first passenger, who had been carrying the Kalashnikov under his coat peered over the metal reinforcement barrier to fire and was instantly shot dead beside me. My windscreen had been shattered and glass was everywhere. I ducked down low and looked through the two holes, keeping my foot right down on the accelerator pedal. I could hear bullets ricocheting off the bus. There was plenty of firing from both sides.

We drove through barricades and men – no matter what was in the way I just carried on. It took only 10 seconds to get through. As soon as we had crossed the border the shooting stopped. I looked up and saw an Austrian armoured carrier parked across the road. I slammed on the brakes just in time.

I felt such a feeling of relief when everyone cheered and shouted, "We've made it!"

One of my passengers spoke German so I asked him to explain who we were and that I was the reporter doing the filming in Budapest.

"We thought you were dead!" the guard said.

"No – I'm alive and kicking," I replied.

Three passengers were dead and others would need an ambulance to take them to hospital. Four were seriously injured.

Things happened very fast afterwards. They took me to Police Headquarters with all my equipment. There was a Hungarian there who spoke to me saying, "It will be very dangerous for you to stay in Europe as there is a price on your head. You have four countries to choose from where you have refugee status – England, America, Canada and South Africa.

I asked if I could have a few minutes to think about it. It didn't take me long. I chose England, as it was closest to Europe, hoping that one day I could return to Hungary.

I was whisked away in a fast car with two guards to Vienna but was too late to catch the last plane to Berlin. It was in the small hours of the morning when we arrived and the last plane had left a few hours ago. The next flight was at 5.00am on 18th December 1956.

I was taken to a hotel to rest and have a meal, where I stayed overnight. I could shower and have the change of clothes given to me. They would not let me wear my long, dark-green greatcoat, which had kept me so warm but now was ready for a clean. I carried it in a bag with me. During the night I had an officer guarding my door and another in an adjoining room.

On the morning of 18th December I was taken to the airport, along with all my equipment and films, and caught the plane to Berlin. I was met at the airport by three plain clothed security men. I handed over everything to them. I was told my plane to England was ready to leave.

Everything was happening so quickly, I could hardly breathe. Just before I boarded the plane an official handed me a large envelope with English money in it.

"Here are two and a half thousand pounds," he said, and shook my hand.

I thanked him.

"It is me who should be thanking you," he replied.

I arrived in England in the late afternoon of the same day. An escort picked me up at the airport and took me to a hotel where over a hundred Hungarian refugees were staying.

They must have heard that someone special was coming but didn't know who. I was told never to tell anyone what I had done, as it was top secret.

When I arrived they greeted me with cheers and shook my hand. I was a hero to them.

But freedom was mine.